DISCRIMINATING YOUR MINDSET

How to Master Your Thoughts, Release What's Holding You Back, and Become Who You Were Meant to Be

SHELLY N. DAVIDSON

Copyright © 2026
SHELLY N. DAVIDSON
DISCRIMINATING YOUR MINDSET
*How to Master Your Thoughts,
Release What's Holding You Back, and
Become Who You Were Meant to Be*
All rights reserved.

No part of this publication may be reproduced, distributed, or transmitted in any form or by any means, including photocopying, recording, or other electronic or mechanical methods, without the prior written permission of the author, except in the case of brief quotations embodied in critical reviews and certain other non-commercial uses permitted by copyright law.

SHELLY N. DAVIDSON

Printed Worldwide
First Printing 2026
First Edition 2026

ISBN: 979-8-9946806-1-2

10 9 8 7 6 5 4 3 2 1

Interior Book Design by Walt's Book Design
www.waltsbookdesign.com

This book is intended for informational and educational purposes only. It does not constitute psychological, medical, legal, or professional advice. The author assumes no responsibility for actions taken by the reader based on the content of this book.

DEDICATION

This book is dedicated to

those who survived what they never speak about,

to those who kept going when clarity felt distant,

and to anyone learning that peace begins

When you choose your thoughts with intention.

You are not behind.

You are becoming.

TABLE OF CONTENTS

FOREWORD

There comes a moment in life when information is no longer enough.

You have read the books.

You have listened to the advice.

You have tried to stay positive, stay strong, and keep going.

And yet—something still feels heavy.

This book was not written to motivate you for a moment. It was written to change the way you relate to your own mind. Because most people are not held back by a lack of knowledge, but by thoughts they never learned to question.

Your life does not move in the direction of your wishes.

It moves in the direction of your dominant thoughts.

Every decision you've delayed, every opportunity you've talked yourself out of, every moment you felt stuck despite knowing better—those moments did not

begin with circumstance. They began with interpretation.

This book introduces a skill most people never develop: **discernment of thought**.

Not every thought is truth.

Not every emotion is instruction.

Not every belief deserves loyalty.

Discriminating Your Mindset is an invitation to slow down, listen carefully, and choose your thoughts with intention. It is a guide for anyone ready to stop fighting their own mind and start living with clarity, peace, and purpose.

Read slowly. Pause when something stirs. Reflect honestly.

This book is not here to push you.

It is here to free you.

INTRODUCTION

THE MOST DANGEROUS PLACE YOU'LL EVER LIVE

If you have ever felt overwhelmed, stuck, or quietly frustrated with your life, there is a truth you may have never heard spoken plainly.

The most dangerous place you will ever live is inside an undisciplined mind.

Not because you are weak.

Not because you lack intelligence, faith, or effort.

But because the mind—when left unchecked—will convince you of things that are not true and present them as facts.

It will speak with confidence.

It will sound logical.

And it will rarely announce itself as fear.

Most people assume their thoughts are trustworthy simply because they are familiar. They believe what feels automatic. They obey what sounds reasonable. And without realizing it, they begin living according to rules they never consciously agreed to.

This is how life becomes smaller without obvious cause.

You start hesitating where you once felt curious.

You begin doubting decisions before you've even made them.

You feel tired—not physically, but mentally—because your mind never rests from negotiation, worry, and second-guessing.

This book is not about controlling your thoughts.

It is about learning how to **choose which ones deserve authority**.

Not every thought is wisdom.

Not every emotion is instruction.

Not every belief is truth.

When the mind lacks discernment, it becomes reactive. It responds to fear as if it were fact. It mistakes familiarity for safety. It convinces you to wait, to delay, to stay small—all in the name of protection.

And yet, nothing about growth has ever been safe.

The purpose of this book is to teach you how to discriminate your mindset—to recognize the difference between thoughts that serve your becoming and thoughts that quietly keep you stuck.

This is not positive thinking. This is not motivation. This is clarity.

As you read, you may begin to notice something subtle but powerful. Certain sentences may slow you down. Certain ideas may feel uncomfortably familiar. That is not coincidence. That is awareness waking up.

Read slowly.

Reflect honestly.

And allow yourself to question what you've always assumed was true.

Because the moment you learn to govern your mind with intention, your life no longer moves by habit.

It moves by choice.

HOW TO USE THIS BOOK

This book is not meant to be rushed.

It was written for moments when something in you is ready to slow down and listen more closely. Read it at a pace that allows ideas to settle rather than pass through. When a sentence causes you to pause, do not move past it too quickly. That pause is part of the work.

You do not need to agree with everything immediately. Discernment begins not with acceptance, but with awareness. Notice what resonates. Notice what challenges you. Notice what feels familiar. Resistance is often information, not a problem to fix.

There is no expectation to read this book in order, and no requirement to finish it quickly. Some chapters may meet you where you are. Others may make sense later. Return to the pages that steady you when your mind feels crowded.

This book is not here to push you forward or tell you who to become. It is here to help you recognize which thoughts deserve your attention and which ones no longer need to lead.

Read honestly. Reflect quietly. And allow clarity to unfold at its own pace.

PART I

AWAKENING AWARENESS

CHAPTER 1

THE WAR YOU DIDN'T KNOW YOU WERE IN

Most people believe life defeats them from the outside.

They point to circumstances, timing, other people, missed opportunities, and unfair outcomes. They blame what is visible because what can be seen feels easier to confront. It feels more manageable to say "If only this had happened differently" than to sit with the possibility that the greatest influence on their life has always been internal.

But long before the world responds to you, something quieter has already decided how you will experience it.

The real war does not begin in events.

It begins in interpretation.

Every single day, you step into life through a mental filter you did not consciously choose. That filter decides what feels threatening and what feels safe, what feels possible and what feels unrealistic, what feels overwhelming and what feels worth pursuing. It shapes your confidence before you speak, your hesitation before you act, and your doubt before you even try.

That filter is your mindset.

You do not experience life as it is.

You experience life as your mind explains it.

And this is where most people lose power without ever realizing they had it.

The mind is designed to protect you. From an evolutionary perspective, it exists to scan for danger, rejection, discomfort, and loss. This protective function is not a flaw — it is biological, necessary, and intelligent. But a mind trained only for survival eventually confuses safety with stagnation.

It begins to favor familiarity over growth.

Predictability over possibility.

Avoidance over expansion.

This is how people stay in lives they secretly want to outgrow.

Research in cognitive psychology shows that the brain relies heavily on automatic thoughts — rapid mental conclusions formed through repetition, emotional memory, and past experiences. These thoughts arrive instantly. They feel instinctive, immediate, and convincing. But instinct does not equal truth.

Automatic thoughts sound like certainty.

"I'm not ready."

"This always happens to me."

"I should wait until I feel more confident."

"It's probably not the right time."

These thoughts do not arrive as questions.

They arrive as statements.

And when statements go unchallenged, they quietly become rules.

Rules about what you attempt.

Rules about what you tolerate.

Rules about how far you allow yourself to go.

This is why people remain stuck in cycles they say they want to escape.

This is why intelligence does not guarantee clarity.

This is why desire alone does not create change.

Because when the mind speaks with confidence, most people obey — without ever realizing they had a choice.

To discriminate your mindset is to interrupt that obedience.

It is the ability to pause between a thought and your belief in it.

Between an emotion and your reaction.

Between fear and decision.

That pause is where power lives.

This is not about suppressing thoughts or pretending fear doesn't exist. Fear will always speak. Doubt will always attempt to protect you from disappointment. The work is not silencing these voices — it is learning which ones deserve authority.

This is discernment.

Some thoughts are guidance.

Some thoughts are habits.

Some thoughts are wounds trying to stay relevant long after the danger has passed.

Until you learn the difference, your life will continue to be shaped by reaction instead of intention.

Most people never realize they are in this war because it doesn't feel violent. It feels familiar. Comfortable. Logical. It sounds responsible. It sounds reasonable. It even sounds wise.

But comfort can be deceptive — especially when it is built on fear disguised as realism.

Fear often introduces itself as caution.

Avoidance often introduces itself as patience.

Stagnation often introduces itself as stability.

And so people wait.

They wait to feel ready.

They wait to feel confident.

They wait for certainty that never comes.

Meanwhile, life keeps moving.

The purpose of this chapter is not to overwhelm you. It is to wake you up gently but honestly. To help you see that the battle you've been fighting is not against circumstance, timing, or fate — it is against unconscious obedience to thoughts you never chose.

Because the moment you realize that your mind has been making decisions on your behalf, you are given back something priceless:

Choice.

And choice is where authorship begins.

Not control.

Not perfection.

Authorship.

The ability to decide what governs you.

The ability to question before obeying.

The ability to live deliberately instead of by default. This chapter is the beginning of that shift.

Chapter 1 Reflection

1. What thoughts do I treat as facts without questioning?
2. Where have I mistaken familiarity for truth?
3. How has my interpretation of events shaped my choices?
4. Where in my life have I been reacting instead of choosing?

Reflection Notes

CHAPTER 2

THE RULES YOU'RE LIVING BY (AND WHO GAVE THEM TO YOU)

Every life operates by rules.

Some are written.

Most are invisible.

These rules shape what you attempt, what you tolerate, what you avoid, and what you quietly believe you deserve. They influence how high you reach, how long you wait, and how quickly you talk yourself out of what you want.

Most people believe they are making free choices.

In reality, many choices are being filtered through rules they never consciously agreed to.

The most powerful rules in your life are not laws, policies, or expectations imposed by the outside world.

They are beliefs.

Beliefs about who you are.

Beliefs about what is possible.

Beliefs about what is safe.

Beliefs about what is appropriate for someone like you.

And here is the unsettling truth: many of the rules governing your life were not chosen. They were absorbed.

They entered quietly. Repeated subtly. Reinforced consistently.

From parents who did the best they could with what they knew.

From teachers who rewarded compliance more than curiosity.

From cultural norms that praised stability while discouraging risk.

From religious interpretations that emphasized restraint over expansion.

From moments when you failed, were rejected, or felt unseen — and quietly decided what that meant about you.

Psychology refers to these as internalized beliefs. Once repeated enough, the brain treats them as facts. Familiarity becomes truth. Comfort becomes authority.

Over time, these beliefs harden into rules.

Rules like:

- Don't aim too high — you'll only be disappointed.
- Stability matters more than fulfillment.
- People like me don't get opportunities like that.
- It's safer to stay where I am.
- It's too late now.

Notice something important.

These rules rarely sound cruel.

They rarely sound dramatic.

They rarely announce themselves as fear.

They sound practical. Responsible. Mature.

They sound like wisdom.

But practicality rooted in fear still limits possibility.

This is why people often defend the very beliefs that restrict them. These rules once offered protection. They reduced risk. They provided explanation during moments of uncertainty or pain.

At one point, believing “I shouldn’t expect too much” may have softened disappointment.

Believing “I need to be realistic” may have helped you survive instability.

Believing “I’ll stay where I’m needed” may have kept relationships intact.

The problem is not that these beliefs existed.

The problem is that they stayed in charge long after their usefulness expired.

A discriminating mindset begins to question internal authority.

Not aggressively.

Not rebelliously.

But honestly.

Who taught me this belief?

What moment cemented it?

Did it protect me once — but limit me now?

Would I still choose this rule if fear were not involved?

Most people never ask these questions. They confuse inheritance with truth. They live under limitations passed down through generations and call it reality.

And the cost is subtle, but profound.

Studies on self-limiting beliefs show that people unconsciously avoid opportunities that conflict with their internal rules — not because they lack desire or ability, but because growth threatens identity.

If struggle defined you, peace feels unfamiliar.

If endurance became your worth, rest feels undeserved.

If chaos was normal, calm feels empty.

If being needed made you valuable, independence feels like abandonment.

This is why change often feels uncomfortable, even when it is good.

You are not just changing circumstances.

You are challenging identity.

And the mind resists identity threats far more than external ones.

This is why people say they want more but hesitate when more becomes available. Why they feel anxious when things start going well. Why they sabotage progress just before momentum builds.

It is not self-destruction.

It is self-protection operating on outdated rules.

Discriminating your mindset does not mean erasing your past or rejecting where you came from. It means examining which rules still deserve authority in your present life.

You are allowed to update beliefs that once kept you safe.

You are allowed to outgrow rules that no longer fit who you are becoming.

This process is not dramatic. It is quiet. It happens in moments when you pause instead of defaulting. When you notice a familiar hesitation and ask yourself, “Whose voice is this?”

When a rule is seen clearly, it loses power.

When a belief is questioned honestly, it softens.

When awareness enters, obedience fades.

And slowly, something shifts.

You stop living by rules you inherited unconsciously.

You start choosing principles intentionally.

That is not rebellion.

That is maturity.

And once you begin choosing your rules consciously, your life stops shrinking quietly.

It begins expanding deliberately.

Chapter 2 Reflection

1. What beliefs do I live by without remembering when I adopted them?
2. Which rules in my life feel protective, but also limiting?
3. Whose voice do I hear when I hesitate?
4. What belief would I choose today if fear were not involved?
5. What part of my identity feels threatened by growth?

Reflection Notes

PART II

BREAKING OLD PATTERNS

CHAPTER 3

WHY YOU KEEP REPEATING WHAT YOU SWORE YOU'D ESCAPE

There is a particular kind of frustration that comes from awareness.

It is not the frustration of ignorance.

It is the frustration of knowing better.

You have reflected.

You have connected the dots.

You have promised yourself—quietly or out loud—that you would not go back.

And yet, you find yourself circling familiar patterns.

Different faces.

Different settings.

Same emotional ending.

This is the moment many people turn inward with anger and shame. They ask questions that cut instead of clarify.

What is wrong with me?

Why do I keep doing this?

Why haven't I learned my lesson by now?

They assume a lack of discipline. A lack of intelligence. A lack of willpower.

But repetition is rarely a moral failure.

It is a neurological one.

The human brain is designed to prioritize familiarity over happiness. Familiarity signals predictability, and predictability signals safety. Long before the mind asks, “Is this good for me?” the nervous system asks, “Is this recognizable?”

And recognizable feels safer than unknown—even when the unknown is healthier.

This is why people return to environments, relationships, and emotional states they consciously

dislike but subconsciously understand. Why they say they want change, but feel anxious when

change actually appears. Why peace can feel unsettling after years of emotional noise.

You do not repeat cycles because you enjoy them.

You repeat them because your nervous system understands them.

Psychological research shows that emotionally charged experiences—especially painful ones—are stored more deeply than logical insight. The brain remembers what hurt before it remembers what made sense. This is why your body often reacts before your mind has time to reason.

You can know something is unhealthy and still feel pulled back toward it.

You can understand a pattern and still find yourself inside it again.

Because knowledge lives in the mind.

Patterns live in the body.

Your brain learned early what pain looked like and built responses to survive it. These responses were not chosen consciously. They were learned quickly, under pressure, when safety mattered more than growth.

Avoidance.

Over-functioning.

People-pleasing.

Emotional withdrawal.

Hyper-independence.

Constant vigilance.

Self-silencing.

These were not flaws.

They were adaptations.

At some point, these strategies protected you. They reduced risk. They helped you navigate uncertainty. They allowed you to function when support was limited or unpredictable.

But survival strategies are not designed to create fulfillment.

They are designed to prevent collapse.

And what once protected you can eventually imprison you.

This is why discriminating your mindset at this stage requires compassion before correction.

You do not heal by shaming patterns that once kept you safe.

You do not break cycles by attacking the part of you that learned how to survive.

You heal by understanding the role these patterns played—and then deciding they no longer get to lead.

This is also why insight alone is not enough.

You can intellectually understand a pattern and still repeat it emotionally. You can explain your behavior perfectly and still feel unable to change it. That does not mean you are failing. It means your nervous system has not yet learned a new experience.

Change happens when understanding is paired with new response.

Each time you pause before reacting, you weaken the old pathway.

Each time you respond differently—even slightly—you strengthen a new one.

Progress here is rarely dramatic.

It is quiet.

Incremental.

Often invisible at first.

It looks like noticing the urge and not judging it.

It looks like choosing a different response and feeling uncomfortable.

It looks like resisting the pull to explain yourself.

It looks like staying present when your instinct is to escape.

And then something unexpected happens.

As patterns loosen, grief appears.

Not because you miss the pain.

But because you are releasing the identity that survived it.

You may grieve the version of yourself who endured.

The version who stayed alert.

The version who adapted so well they forgot how to rest.

This grief can feel confusing. You may wonder why letting go feels heavy when it's supposed to feel freeing.

But this grief is not regression.

It is transition.

It is the nervous system learning that it no longer has to stay braced.

It is the mind releasing an identity it once needed.

It is the body adjusting to a life with less threat.

And if you allow it—without rushing it, fixing it, or explaining it away—this grief becomes the gateway to freedom.

Because repetition ends not when you force yourself to change, but when safety is redefined.

Not safety as familiarity.

But safety as presence.

Safety as choice.

Safety as self-trust.

This chapter is not here to fix you.

It is here to remind you that nothing about you is broken.

You adapted.

You survived.

And now, you are learning how to live beyond survival.

Chapter 3 Reflection

1. What patterns continue to repeat in my life, even though I understand them?
    - What might these patterns have once protected me from?
    - How do I typically respond to myself when I notice repetition?
2. What would it feel like to meet this pattern with curiosity instead of judgment?
    - What small pause could I practice before reacting?

Reflection Notes

CHAPTER 4

THE WEIGHT YOU LEARNED TO CARRY WITHOUT REALIZING IT

Most people do not realize they are carrying emotional weight until their mind gets tired.

Not physically tired.

Not situationally tired.

But deeply, internally exhausted.

The kind of exhaustion that sleep does not fix.

The kind that makes peace feel unfamiliar.

The kind that lingers even when life appears stable.

This exhaustion is confusing because it doesn't always match what is happening on the outside. You may be functioning well. Showing up. Meeting expectations. Holding things together. And yet, something inside you feels heavy, dull, or strained

That weight does not come from one dramatic moment.

It accumulates quietly.

It builds when emotions are postponed instead of processed.

When grief is minimized because others "have it worse."

When anger is swallowed to keep the peace.

When disappointment is dismissed because "that's just life."

When fear is silenced because "I can't fall apart right now."

You learn to function.

You learn to cope.

You learn to move on.

But moving on is not the same as laying things down.

Psychology tells us that unprocessed emotions do not disappear. They remain active in the nervous system, influencing perception, decision-making, and emotional regulation long after the original event has passed. The mind may move forward, but the body keeps the record.

This is why people feel anxious without a clear reason.

Irritable without a clear trigger.

Numb when they want to feel alive.

Tense even when nothing is wrong.

The mind keeps records the heart never had time to review.

Many people mistake this weight for personal weakness. They assume something is wrong with them because they can't "get over" what they've already survived. But the truth is simpler — and kinder.

You were not given space to feel.

You were rewarded for being strong.

Praised for holding it together.

Relied on for being dependable.

Needed for being capable.

So you learned a quiet lesson:

Your value came from endurance.

Discriminating your mindset at this stage means learning the difference between strength and suppression.

You were strong for surviving.

You were resilient for enduring.

But you do not have to keep proving strength by carrying everything forever.

There is a subtle pressure many people live under — the pressure to be okay. To not burden others. To not dwell too long. To not fall apart. To keep moving. To stay productive. To remain functional.

Over time, this pressure becomes internalized.

You stop checking in with yourself.

You stop asking how you actually feel.

You stop noticing when your body tightens or your breath shortens.

Instead, you tell yourself things that sound reasonable:

"It wasn't that bad."

"I should be over this by now."

"I don't have time to unpack all that."

"Other people handled worse."

These thoughts don't come from cruelty.

They come from adaptation.

But the body does not forget what the mind avoids.

Unprocessed pain shows up subtly. It shows up as hesitation when you want confidence. Guardedness when you want closeness. Overthinking when you want peace. Difficulty trusting joy. An inability to fully relax even in safe moments.

The nervous system remains alert, even when there is no immediate threat.

This is not because you are broken.

It is because your system learned to stay ready.

Healing does not begin with reliving everything you've been through.

It does not require dramatizing pain or reopening wounds.

Healing begins with acknowledgment.

Not analysis.

Not justification.

Not comparison.

Acknowledgment.

Naming what you carried.

Honoring the impact it had.

Allowing yourself to say, "That mattered."

When you acknowledge what you carried, the weight begins to shift. Not because everything is suddenly resolved, but because you are no longer pretending nothing happened.

This is emotional honesty.

And emotional honesty creates space.

Space to breathe differently.

Space to respond instead of brace.

Space to feel without being overwhelmed.

You do not have to collapse to lay things down.

You do not have to fall apart to be honest.

Sometimes healing looks like quietly admitting, "That was heavier than I realized."

And in that admission, something loosens.

This chapter is not asking you to reopen pain.

It is inviting you to stop carrying it alone.

Because the weight you've been holding was never meant to define you — only to be acknowledged, understood, and eventually released.

Chapter 4 Reflection

1. What emotions have I learned to minimize or ignore?
2. Where in my body do I feel heaviness that words haven't reached yet?
3. What experiences did I move past without having space to feel?
4. How have I confused strength with suppression?
5. What would it look like to acknowledge what I carried — without Judgment?

Reflection Notes

CHAPTER 5

WHO ARE YOU WITHOUT THE STRUGGLE?

When you begin to lay emotional weight down, something unexpected often happens.

There is space.

Not relief yet.

Not joy.

Just space.

And for many people, that space feels unfamiliar — even unsettling.

Because for so long, your inner world was occupied by responsibility, vigilance, endurance, and effort. When those demands soften, the mind asks a quiet but profound question:

Who am I now?

For many people, struggle becomes more than a season.

It becomes an identity.

You are the strong one.

The responsible one.

The survivor.

The one who holds it together when others can't.

These identities were not chosen out of ego.

They were formed out of necessity.

At some point, being strong kept things moving.

Being resilient kept you safe.

Being self-reliant kept you standing when support was limited or unreliable.

These identities deserve respect.

But survival identities — while essential in one season — can quietly limit growth in the next.

Psychological research on identity formation shows that people often cling to roles that once protected them, even when those roles no longer serve their present life. Not because they want to suffer — but because identity provides continuity. It answers the question "Who am I?" when everything else feels uncertain.

If pain shaped your sense of purpose, peace can feel unfamiliar.

If endurance became your value, ease can feel undeserved.

If chaos was normal, calm can feel empty.

This is why healing can feel disorienting.

You are not just releasing pain.

You are releasing definition.

Discriminating your mindset here requires a quieter form of courage — the courage to loosen your grip on what once defined you without needing to replace it immediately.

You are not dishonoring your past by choosing a lighter future.

You are honoring it by refusing to remain trapped there.

Growth does not erase meaning.

It integrates it.

Post-traumatic growth research shows that people who intentionally redefine themselves after hardship experience deeper fulfillment than those who simply "return to normal." Healing is not about going back to who you were before the struggle.

It is about moving forward with greater awareness, flexibility, and self-trust.

You do not need to stay hardened to stay authentic.

You do not need to struggle to stay worthy.

You do not need pain to justify your existence.

As this truth settles — slowly, unevenly — your internal questions begin to change.

You stop asking:

"How do I get through this?"

And start asking:

"How do I want to live?"

That question marks the transition from survival to authorship.

And authorship requires something new — not force, not pressure, not constant effort — but discipline rooted in self-respect rather than fear.

That is where we go next.

Chapter 5 Reflection

1. How much of my identity has been shaped by survival rather than choice?
2. What feels unfamiliar — or even uncomfortable — about peace?
3. Who might I become if struggle no longer defined me?
4. What am I afraid to release because it has always felt familiar?
5. What does authorship mean to me at this stage of my life?

Reflection Notes

PART III

BUILDING SELF-RESPECT AND CLARITY

CHAPTER 6

DISCIPLINE IS SELF-RESPECT IN MOTION

When you begin to release struggle as an identity, something subtle but powerful shifts.

You stop forcing yourself forward.

You stop negotiating with exhaustion.

You stop relying on pressure to move.

And in that quiet space, a new question emerges:

How do I take care of the life I am choosing?

This is where discipline enters — not as punishment, not as control, but as care.

Discipline has a reputation it does not deserve.

For many people, the word carries the weight of pressure, rigidity, correction, or failure. It feels like something imposed — by parents, institutions, religion, or circumstances. Something you submit to when you fall short rather than something you choose when you respect yourself.

But true discipline is none of those things.

Discipline is not force.

It is not denial.

It is not cruelty disguised as productivity.

Discipline is self-respect made visible.

It is the quiet decision to honor the person you are becoming, even when the version of you today feels tired, uncertain, or unmotivated. It is not about rejecting rest or joy. It is about choosing alignment over impulse — not because you are afraid, but because you care.

Psychology is clear on this: motivation is unreliable. It rises and falls with mood, energy, stress, and environment. Discipline, however, creates structure — and structure creates safety.

When your mind knows what to expect from you, it relaxes.

It stops negotiating.

It stops bracing.

A discriminating mindset understands this distinction.

You stop asking, "Do I feel like it?"

And start asking, "Does this align with who I am becoming?"

That shift changes your relationship with yourself.

Discipline does not demand perfection.

It asks for consistency.

It asks for follow-through on small, repeatable commitments. Each time you keep a promise to yourself — however minor — you repair trust. And over time, that trust becomes confidence.

Not the loud kind that performs.

The grounded kind that doesn't need validation.

This is why discipline feels stabilizing when it is rooted in self-respect. It reduces internal conflict. It quiets the constant bargaining between intention and comfort. It gives your mind evidence that you are reliable.

You are no longer convincing yourself to believe in you.

You are showing yourself.

Discriminating your mindset here means separating discipline from shame.

You are not behind because you struggled.

You are not weak because growth took time.

You are not failing because consistency came slowly.

Discipline simply asks one question:

What is one action today that honors the life I am building?

And when you answer that question consistently — without drama, without punishment —

identity begins to shift.

You stop trying to become disciplined.

You become someone who follows through.

But discipline cannot flourish in an environment that continually drains you — internally or externally. Respect without protection erodes over time.

Which is why the next skill is essential.

Chapter 6 Reflection

1. Where do my current actions contradict my stated values?
2. What promises have I been breaking with myself — and why?
3. What is one small, realistic commitment I can honor today?
4. How would my life feel if I trusted myself again?
5. What does self-respect look like in action, not intention?

Reflection Notes

CHAPTER 7

BOUNDARIES ARE THE LANGUAGE OF SELF-RESPECT

When you begin to practice discipline rooted in self-respect, something becomes clear very quickly.

Not everything in your life supports that respect.

Some demands drain it.

Some relationships dilute it.

Some expectations quietly undo the care you are trying to give yourself.

This is where boundaries become necessary — not as walls, but as definitions.

Boundaries are often misunderstood as distance or rejection.

In reality, they are clarity.

They define what is yours to carry and what is not.

They define what you will tolerate and what you will no longer absorb.

They define how you protect your peace without apology.

Many people struggle with boundaries not because they lack strength, but because they fear disconnection.

They worry that saying no will cost them love.

That choosing themselves will appear selfish.

That limits will create distance or disappointment.

So they over-explain.

Over-give.

Over-extend.

They hope generosity will secure connection.

But the absence of boundaries does not create closeness.

It creates resentment.

Psychological research consistently shows that people with weak boundaries experience higher levels of stress, burnout, and emotional fatigue. Not because they care too much — but because

they care without discrimination.

They say yes when their body is asking for rest.

They absorb emotions that are not theirs to manage.

They carry responsibility for outcomes they cannot control.

A discriminating mindset learns to pause before responding and ask quieter, more honest questions:

Does this demand align with my values?

Does this relationship nourish me — or deplete me?

Am I saying yes out of intention — or fear?

Boundaries are not punishment.

They are honesty.

They allow you to show up fully without abandoning yourself. They protect your mental and emotional space so your thoughts are not constantly crowded with obligations that do not belong to you.

When you begin setting boundaries, discomfort often comes first.

Not because boundaries are wrong — but because people who benefited from your lack of boundaries may resist the change.

You may feel guilt.

You may feel anxiety.

You may feel the urge to explain, justify, or retreat.

That discomfort is temporary.

The peace that follows is lasting.

As boundaries take shape, something subtle but powerful happens.

Your energy returns.

Your internal dialogue quiets.

You stop rehearsing conversations that haven't happened yet.

You stop explaining yourself to people who aren't listening.

You begin to live from intention rather than reaction.

Boundaries are not about controlling others.

They are about clarifying yourself.

They tell the world how to treat you — not through demand, but through consistency.

And when boundaries support discipline, and discipline supports self-respect, something stabilizes.

Your life becomes quieter.

Clearer.

Less fragmented.

That internal stability prepares you for the next transformation — one that determines whether clarity becomes fleeting or sustainable.

Your ability to focus.

Chapter 7 Reflection

1. Where in my life do I feel consistently drained or resentful?
2. What emotions surface when I consider setting a boundary?
3. Who benefits when I do not protect my energy?
4. What boundary would create peace rather than distance?
5. How would my life change if I trusted that honesty is kinder than over-giving?

Reflection Notes

CHAPTER 8

FOCUS IS PRESENCE, NOT PRESSURE

When you begin setting boundaries, something subtle happens.

Your life grows quieter.

Not empty — quieter.

The constant pull eases.

The internal noise softens.

The sense of being pulled in too many directions begins to loosen.

And in that quiet, something becomes possible again.

Focus.

But not the kind of focus most people have been taught to chase.

Focus has been reduced to productivity.

Do more.

Move faster.

Keep up.

This version of focus is exhausting — and ultimately ineffective. It asks the mind to perform while never allowing it to settle. It turns attention into pressure and presence into urgency.

Real focus is not pressure.

It is presence.

Presence with what matters.

Presence with what you are building.

Presence with yourself.

We live in a world designed to fracture attention. Notifications, comparison, urgency, and noise compete constantly for the mind. Neuroscience shows that chronic distraction weakens emotional regulation and decision-making. Over time, a distracted mind becomes an anxious mind — not because life is worse, but because the nervous system never settles.

When attention is always divided, the body never receives the signal that it is safe to rest.

A discriminating mindset begins to protect attention as something valuable — not something to spend recklessly.

Because attention determines what grows.

Whatever you repeatedly focus on gains emotional weight.

Fear grows when rehearsed.

Gratitude grows when noticed.

Anxiety grows when the mind lives everywhere except the present moment.

This is why distraction is not neutral.

It shapes identity.

When attention is scattered, identity becomes scattered. You feel pulled in multiple directions, uncertain of priorities, disconnected from intuition. Decisions feel urgent instead of intentional. Rest feels unproductive instead of necessary.

You may find yourself busy but unsatisfied.

Occupied but unfulfilled.

Moving constantly but arriving nowhere.

Discriminating your mindset here means learning to slow your mental pace without guilt.

You stop equating busyness with worth.

You stop measuring progress by speed.

You stop filling silence just to avoid discomfort.

Focus becomes an act of self-trust.

You choose to be fully present with the task, conversation, or moment in front of you — not

because nothing else matters, but because this moment does.

Presence restores depth.

Depth restores calm.

And when you are truly present, your nervous system receives a message it has been waiting for:

I am safe right now.

That message changes everything.

Thoughts slow.

Breathing deepens.

Clarity sharpens without effort.

In that calm, something quiet but powerful begins to surface.

Hope.

Not the loud kind built on optimism or promises.

The steady kind built on presence.

The kind that says: If I can be here, I can move forward.

And from that place, the future no longer feels overwhelming.

It feels possible.

Chapter 8 Reflection

1. What most often fragments my attention throughout the day?
2. How does constant distraction affect my emotional state and sense of clarity?
3. Where do I confuse urgency with importance?
4. What would it feel like to give my full presence to one thing today?
5. What signals does my body send when I finally slow down?

Reflection Notes

PART IV

CHOOSING FORWARD

CHAPTER 9

HOPE IS STRENGTH WHEN YOU'RE TIRED

After presence comes something fragile.

Not clarity.

Not certainty.

But a quiet openness.

When the mind finally settles, it becomes aware of how tired it has been. And in that awareness, hope often feels distant — not because it is gone, but because exhaustion has been speaking for so long.

Hope is often misunderstood.

It is mistaken for optimism.

For positive thinking.

For pretending things are better than they are.

But real hope is not cheerful denial.

It is grounded endurance.

Hope does not say, "Everything will be fine."

Hope says, "This is not the end."

Psychological research consistently shows that hope is one of the strongest predictors of resilience. People who retain hope adapt more effectively, persist longer through difficulty, and recover more fully from adversity — not because they ignore reality, but because they believe reality is still unfolding.

Hope allows room for uncertainty without collapsing into despair.

A discriminating mindset understands that hopeless thoughts often arrive when energy is depleted.

"This won't change."

"I've already tried."

"This is just how my life is."

These thoughts feel convincing because exhaustion narrows perspective. It limits imagination. It reduces the mind's ability to see alternatives. Fatigue confuses temporary limitation with permanent truth.

Hopelessness is often not insight.

It is fatigue speaking.

Hope widens the lens.

It does not erase pain — it holds it without surrendering to it.

It does not rush healing — it allows rest without giving up.

It does not demand certainty — it creates space for possibility.

Hope says: "I don't need to know how yet."

Hope says: "I can move slowly."

Hope says: "Something is still forming."

Hope does not require confidence.

It requires courage.

The courage to believe growth can be happening quietly.

The courage to trust that clarity can return.

The courage to keep going without guarantees.

Discriminating your mindset here means learning to question despair the same way you learned to question fear.

You pause and ask:

Am I truly out of options — or am I tired?

Is this conclusion accurate — or is it asking for rest?

What would it mean to believe this season is shaping me, not ending me?

Hope does not pull you forward by force.

It sits with you until your strength returns.

And when it does, movement becomes possible again — not frantic, not forced, but steady.

Hope is not loud.

It is patient.

And when you honor it, even gently, it becomes enough.

Chapter 9 Reflection

1. Where have I mistaken exhaustion for truth?
2. What thoughts tend to appear when my energy is lowest?
3. How does hope feel different from optimism in my body?
4. What would hope look like without certainty or pressure?
5. What part of my future still feels quietly possible?

Reflection Notes

CHAPTER 10

THE DAY YOU STOP WAITING FOR PERMISSION

There is a quiet moment in every life when something shifts.

It is not loud.

It is not dramatic.

There is no announcement.

You simply realize you are done waiting.

Not waiting because you are impatient.

Not waiting because you are reckless.

Waiting because, for a long time, it felt safer than choosing.

Waiting to feel ready.

Waiting to be chosen.

Waiting for clarity, validation, closure, or approval.

At first, waiting felt responsible. Wise. Mature. You told yourself you were being patient — and sometimes you were. There are seasons where waiting is necessary, even protective.

But eventually, something changes.

Waiting stops being discernment.

It becomes delay.

Psychology refers to this as decision avoidance — a pattern where the mind convinces itself that not choosing is neutral. But not choosing is never neutral. Over time, it quietly teaches you to trust hesitation more than instinct.

You begin to doubt your own readiness.

You wait for conditions that never fully arrive.

You postpone movement while calling it preparation.

A discriminating mindset recognizes the moment when waiting is no longer wisdom.

Growth does not ask for permission.

It asks for participation.

The people who move forward are not the ones who feel the most confident. They are the ones who accept that clarity often arrives after movement, not before it.

This chapter is not about forcing action.

It is about reclaiming authorship.

You stop asking, “What if this doesn’t work?”

And start asking, “What if staying still costs me more?”

You begin to understand that forward motion does not require certainty — only honesty. Honest acknowledgment that you are no longer the person you were when waiting made sense.

So you move.

Not recklessly.

Not dramatically.

But deliberately.

One decision.

One boundary.

One conversation.

One step aligned with who you are now.

And once you move, something subtle but powerful happens.

You begin to trust yourself in motion.

Not because everything works out immediately — but because you prove to yourself that you can choose without abandoning yourself.

Waiting taught you how to endure.

Choosing teaches you how to live.

Chapter 10 Reflection

1. Where am I waiting out of habit rather than intention?
2. What decision have I been postponing because it feels uncomfortable or uncertain?
3. What would it look like to move forward imperfectly but honestly?
4. What permission am I still waiting for — and who am I hoping will give it?
5. How might my life change if I trusted myself to decide?

Reflection Notes

CHAPTER 11

PEACE IS WHAT HAPPENS WHEN YOU STOP FIGHTING YOURSELF

Peace is not the absence of struggle.

It is the absence of inner war.

For many people, life is not loud with conflict — it is quiet with tension. A constant, low-grade strain beneath the surface. The effort of holding competing truths at the same time.

Who you are

versus

who you think you should be.

What you feel

versus

what you believe is acceptable to feel.

What your body knows

versus

what your mind insists on controlling.

This internal conflict is exhausting.

Psychological studies show that prolonged inner tension keeps the nervous system in a persistent state of alert. Even when nothing is wrong externally, the body remains braced. Muscles stay tight. Breathing stays shallow. Thoughts stay vigilant.

This is why rest can feel uncomfortable.

Why stillness can feel unsafe.

Why peace can feel unfamiliar — even threatening.

A discriminating mindset begins to recognize that peace does not come from control.

It comes from alignment.

Alignment between values and actions.

Alignment between boundaries and relationships.

Alignment between inner truth and outer life.

Alignment is not perfection.

It is honesty.

As alignment grows, self-betrayal fades.

You stop forcing yourself to fit spaces you've outgrown.

You stop rehearsing conversations that no longer need to happen.

You stop living in defense mode — bracing for impact that never comes.

Peace does not mean you never feel fear, sadness, or doubt.

It means those emotions no longer lead.

They are felt — but not obeyed.

Acknowledged — but not amplified.

This is where rest becomes real.

Not collapse.

Not avoidance.

Not numbing.

But grounded rest.

Rest that allows the nervous system to settle without shutting down.

Rest that feels spacious instead of heavy.

Rest that does not require distraction to tolerate.

You begin to sit with yourself without judgment.

To experience silence without panic.

To breathe without urgency.

The need to prove, defend, or perform softens.

You are no longer negotiating with yourself.

No longer divided against your own needs.

No longer living as if peace must be earned.

You are not fighting yourself anymore.

And when that fight ends, something fundamental changes.

Life does not suddenly become easy — but it becomes clear.

Challenges still arise — but they are met, not resisted.

Movement continues — but without force.

Peace becomes the ground you stand on, not the reward you chase.

Chapter 11 Reflection

1. Where in my life do I still feel internal tension or resistance?
2. What part of me am I trying to control instead of understand?
3. Where am I out of alignment with my own values or needs?
4. What would it feel like to stop arguing with myself?
5. How does peace show up when I allow it rather than pursue it?

Reflection Notes

CHAPTER 12

YOU ARE ALLOWED TO BEGIN AGAIN

After the inner war quiets, something simple becomes possible.

Choice.

Not the frantic kind driven by urgency or fear.

The grounded kind that rises when you are no longer arguing with yourself.

Many people carry a quiet belief they rarely question:

If I move on, it means what happened didn't matter.

This belief keeps them tethered to the past long after its lessons have been learned. It confuses remembrance with loyalty. It mistakes release for erasure.

But beginning again does not erase meaning.

It honors growth.

You do not begin again because the past was insignificant.

You begin again because you have carried it as far as it can go.

Healing is not forgetting.

It is remembering without reliving.

Psychological research shows that healing occurs when emotional charge decreases — not when memory disappears. You remember without returning. You acknowledge without reopening wounds. The past becomes information, not instruction.

A discriminating mindset allows this.

You stop demanding that pain justify its continued presence.

You stop asking suffering to explain itself.

You stop measuring worth by endurance alone.

You choose a new measure.

Clarity.

Peace.

Forward motion.

Beginning again does not require a dramatic reinvention.

It does not require erasing who you were or pretending you are untouched.

It requires honesty.

Honesty about what you have outgrown.

Honesty about what no longer needs to be carried.

Honesty about the person you are becoming.

You are allowed to want more without apology.

You are allowed to rest without explanation.

You are allowed to grow without permission.

You are not behind.

You are not broken.

You are not late to your own life.

You are becoming.

And becoming does not need noise.

It needs faithfulness.

Faithfulness to your values.

Faithfulness to your limits.

Faithfulness to the quiet knowing that now lives inside you.

So begin again.

Not as someone new —

but as someone truer.

Carry what matters.

Release what doesn't.

And walk forward lighter than before.

Chapter 12 Reflection

1. What am I ready to release without guilt or justification?
2. What lessons am I carrying forward — and which burdens can stay behind?
3. Who am I choosing to be from this place of clarity?
4. What does beginning again look like quietly, not dramatically?
5. How can I honor my past without living inside it?

Reflection Notes

CLOSING PRAYER / AFFIRMATION

I release the thoughts that no longer serve my healing.

The thoughts rooted in fear, comparison, urgency, and self-doubt.

I loosen my grip on stories that kept me small when I was only trying to survive.

I allow my mind to soften where it once stayed rigid.

I forgive myself for surviving the best way I knew how.

For the choices I made when clarity was limited.

For the strength I had to carry before I knew how to rest.

For the ways I adapted, endured, and protected myself when safety felt uncertain.

I honor who I was without trapping myself there.

I acknowledge what I carried without asking it to define me.

I thank every version of myself that got me here.

I choose clarity over chaos.

Not because life is perfect, but because my inner world deserves honesty.

I choose intention over fear, even when fear still speaks.

I choose presence over pressure, truth over performance, alignment over approval.

I release the need to rush my becoming.

I release the belief that I am behind.

I release the weight of proving, explaining, and earning rest.

I am not late.

I am not broken.

I am not unfinished.

I am becoming — steadily, faithfully, quietly.

As I move forward, I trust that my mind can learn peace.

Not by force, but by compassion.

Not by control, but by understanding.

I trust that my heart can learn rest.

Rest that is safe.

Rest that is honest.

Rest that does not require collapse or escape.

I trust that my life can unfold with purpose.

Not all at once.

Not without challenge.

But with meaning, integrity, and direction.

I allow myself to begin again without guilt.

To grow without permission.

To live without constant defense.

May I listen more closely to what is true.

May I move forward without abandoning myself.

May I carry what matters — and release what no longer belongs to me.

And may the life I build from here

be shaped by clarity, guided by peace,

and grounded in self-respect.

Amen.

DAILY AFFIRMATION

Today, I release thoughts that no longer serve my healing.

I honor the ways I survived and forgive myself for what I did not know then.

I choose clarity over chaos.

I choose intention over fear.

I am not late.

I am not broken.

I am becoming.

I trust my mind can learn peace,

my heart can learn rest,

and my life can unfold with purpose.

Today, I move forward gently,

faithful to who I am becoming

DAILY ANCHORS

Mantras for Morning, Anxiety, Transition, and Rest

Morning

Today, I move with clarity, intention, and self-respect.

When Anxiety Rises

I am safe in this moment, and I do not need to rush my becoming.

During Transition

I release what no longer fits and trust what is unfolding.

When Doubt Appears

I do not need permission to grow into who I am becoming.

When Rest Is Needed

Rest is allowed, and peace is productive for me.

End of Day

I did enough today, and I am allowed to rest.

A FINAL NOTE TO THE READER

If you have made it this far, nothing about you is accidental.

You did not read this book because you needed fixing.

You read it because something in you was ready to listen more closely.

There is no requirement to rush what comes next.

No expectation to transform overnight.

No pressure to prove that this reading "worked."

What matters is not what you do immediately after this book,

but how you treat yourself moving forward.

Return to these pages when you need steadiness.

Return to the anchors when your mind feels crowded.

Return to yourself when the world feels loud.

You are allowed to move slowly.

You are allowed to change quietly.

You are allowed to live without constant explanation.

Whatever unfolds next does not need to be dramatic to be meaningful.

It only needs to be honest.

And that honesty—when practiced gently—will carry you forward.

NOTES

NOTES

NOTES

NOTES

NOTES

NOTES

NOTES

NOTES

NOTES

NOTES

NOTES

NOTES

www.ingramcontent.com/pod-product-compliance
Lightning Source LLC
LaVergne TN
LVHW011047110826
845149LV00015B/3391